Once More With
Noise

poems by

Weasel

Once More with Noise
Weasel

ISBN-13: 978-1-948712-77-4

© 2020 Weasel
Front Cover Image by Joseph Chou

Printed in the U.S.A.

Weasel Press
Lansing, MI
http://www.weaselpress.com

https://degenerateweasel.weebly.com
https://queerweasel.blogspot.com

ALL RIGHTS RESERVED. This book contains material protected under International and Federal Copyright Laws and Treaties. Any unauthorized reprint or use of this material is prohibited. No part of this book, or use of characters in this book, may be reproduced or transmitted in any form or by any means, electronic or mechanical, including photocopying, recording, or by any information storage and retrieval system without express written permission from the author / publisher.

Contents

the minotaur   1

I

my notebook is a weasel   5
toss me to the waiting sky   7
my mother told me not to write
    another poem about her   10
my therapist asked me what it's like
    when i think of killing myself   13
fat shaming   14
my skull is all booked up   16
shit your therapist tells you but you don't believe   19

II

mary oliver said her lover gave her a box of darkness   25
we were the calm before disaster   27
the day i met my former father-in-law   29
my ex says some people woke up
    on the wrong side of the world   31
my ex tells me to be more tolerant   32
you texted me drunk   35
when your ex says he's sorry   37
i had a therapist that said he was gonna fuck me up   39
clive barker taught me fear is everywhere   42

III

buddy wakefield taught me to look   47
the baker talks to himself while waiting   49
orion hunts in the swamps of texas   51
sylvia plath says dying is an art   52
they like to call when the sun ain't out   54

the ghost of donations long past	55
my mother died when she wished her children normal	57

IV

virginia woolf steals the window in my home	61
the enchantment of the ordinary	62
i'll be damned if i didn't hit a fuckin' pole	64
we drove through arkansas	65
when a texan first sees snow	66
when poseidon drinks	68
charon likes to get out	70

V

bukowski taught me how to fuck	75
i read a poem about eating your ass to my friends	78
the sun was setting as we left port	80
what if i never get rid of you	81
arthur c. clarke taught me how to wonder	82
you put the brightest star on top	84
we kissed beneath a streetlight	86

outro

healing is a slit throat waiting to sing	89

Content Warning

This book contains themes of domestic violence, homophobia, suicidal ideation, sexual content, and racism.

To Jonny

Therapist: That's called abuse. And that's not okay.

There was silence for a moment. Maybe two. I don't process things immediately. I need a minute to let the words roll around in my head before I can go, "ok. I hear you." So, I let the words roll.

Therapist: What are you thinking right now?

My skull is always filled with noise. It's hard for me to push through it sometimes; hard for me to focus.

Me: I hear what you're saying. My brain is kind of raging right now. It's just buzzing. So much buzzing. I know I don't want it to be true.

Therapist: Why don't you want that to be true?

Why he always gotta ask the hard questions? I guess that's what they get paid to do. I didn't have an answer that day. But now I believe it's because I wasn't ready to touch that trauma yet. I wasn't ready to look at it in the face. Yes, I know the signs of abuse. Yes, I know getting thrown into walls every which way but fuckin' Sunday is abuse. I know all that.

I'm a domestic abuse survivor.

But that don't mean I'm ready to confront it. Since that session months back, I started poking at this book. Originally going to be 80 poems, but I cut it short. An author knows when their manuscript is done. And I'm tired.

Before you jump into this book, know that my way of processing my trauma, of figuring out the world, of breathing, all of that is done through poetry. *Once More with Noise* is my way of navigating the waters of my trauma. It's not an easy read.

I wish I could say it was rough writing it, and to some extent it was. But seeing everything again was like feeling numb when you see a photograph. And I'm tired of being numb.

Once More with Noise is incendiary. Filled to the brim with embers that I don't know if I can put out on my own. I'm trying. Everyone says handling your own trauma is tough, but they never say how much it weighs on you. It's not something you can tuck away and deal with later. I've tried it. That don't work. There's not a day I don't feel it. It's why I like loud noise. Air condition units, metal music, fans, white noise, anything to keep my brain from running and running and running.

Much like *Cut the Loss* before this, take this book for what it is.

Once More with Noise

the minotaur

and what mercy should you have to those who
called you a beast at birth? you who are no
more monster than they are. devour them
all because beasts are only as natural
as the beds they sleep in. they dream to slay
you, dream of grabbing you by the horns and
driving their swords into your throat. yet you
are a god, much like poseidon. not beast—

bull without name, you are a war dripping
with rage and carnality. why remain
chaste when the urge lingers in your belly?
though you think appetites are impulsive,
they return furiously. so, when man
arrives, satiate your sins, and go mad.

I

my notebook is a weasel

is a river of words
carried in broken
throats & fuzzy skulls

izzy don't sleep
so good
always tired
yet restless
in bed

asks me if i
see snow
outside

& i say "yea...
it's melting"

he stares
out the window
eyes filled
with grief

"did you ever think
it'd be so ugly
when it melts"

& i start coffee
because sleep
will not fall
from the moon

izzy counts the books

on our shelf
as if counting
sheep

but he can't
keep focus

dances fake
kung fu
to a song
only he knows
while getting
lost between
ginsberg & virgil

& when i pour
the pot, i open
him up

because restless
nights are like
slit throats

they still pour
words from
their wounds

toss me to the waiting sky

my tongue is
bundled with
apologies

spilling at the
first sign of
wreckage

they drizzle from my lips
like syrup from the jar

when you are a graveyard
of anxiety, no one tells you
how easy it is to stop
the river along your bones

it's been 90 days since
i last thought of
killing myself

the first thing i did today
while making coffee
was dream

sun shut out by the blinds
i dreamt i walked
into the sky

dreamt my spirit
left flesh behind
in search of air
less painful to breathe

and then worry asks if
i think i am ready

and like the coffee
spills from the pot
i tell the air i'm sorry
because anxiety is a bad lover

he pushes you just
far enough to keep
your focus on him

anxiety wants you to go
but only when he loosens
his grasp around your neck

when living with panic
you have to stay grounded
even when the sky
looks gorgeous

even when it waits
for you to dance
into its patient arms

we all last forever

only

forever is a lifetime—
expiration dates
lie dormant
until they want

to drop

some days i feel
my last breath
coming, running
down the street,
aiming its best wishes
and goodbye psalms
at me

i have waltzed
with him before

taken his hand
in mine and used
my calloused feet
to swing to the sky

he whispers in my ear
that i am ready to fly
and i hold him as if
holding a lover

only

i don't feel
my wings

my mother told me not to write another poem about her

i am your martyr, boy
every painful truth
you write down
on paper is
another cut to
my flesh

i was never the good mom
but you can at least
recognize my
sadness

and
forgive

because i told you
to forgive

because i am
your mother (martyr)

and i've done
so much to
make you

to mold you

you fill your books
with my faults

i am faultless
in your eyes

boy

remember that

remember that i
take up space
in your skull
because i'm
supposed to

you will not
shove me out
like you did
your father

i am better
than that

and i will fight you
like how you
fight me
when i tell
you your
gay is too much

tone it down
be conservative

you're a man
goddammit

act
like
it

and keep me
out of
your books

because my
martyrdom
works best
in shadows

my therapist asked me what it's like when i think of killing myself

i can feel
the gun
pressed hard
against my head

i'm sitting in my car
and an ocean
hangs above me

the air has
never felt
so silent

and i think

i'm ready
i'm ready
i'm ready

finger shaky
i feel it
pull the
trigger

and then
i wake up

fat shaming

i feel it in my cheeks
after eating

like puffed out
sludge hanging
on my face

it's like my
brain can't
shut it off

this feeling of
grossness
oozing along
my body
as i dissect
everything
i consumed

some days
i am weak

unable to
pin down
the voices
rattling off

they—the firing
squad mouthing
bullets into
all the wrong parts
of myself

i've yet to
stop them

what is there
to stop
when you
love yourself
only enough
to live?

my skull is all booked up

inhabited with problems
dressed as people

they like to argue
start shit when
i'm most relaxed
(vulnerable)

because who needs
to relax when
they're watching you

my mom pushes for
me to be the more
conservative gay
because feeling
like not knowing
her son is gay
is better than
knowing her
son is

gay

and we argue
over this
as if she
were here
in my living room

my ex berates me
about the divorce

paperwork like
a meek mouse

and we argue
all of his
complaints
bubbling back
as if he
were right
inside my ear

they like
to hit me
in the morning
as i sit
with my coffee
and stare at
the stone clouds
hovering in
michigan sky

my tenants know
when i am exhausted

know that
i won't fight
back hard
because
tired
holds firm
in a body

we will resolve

nothing

allowing them
to take another
month of space
without paying rent

and why should
they pay rent
if i am the issue

only

i'm not so
certain
who is at fault
anymore

shit your therapist tells you but you don't believe

you'll be
talkin'

each word a
new step
up as if
ascending
through old
photographs

your feet will
slip, you'll
plummet down
and have to
redo progress

but that's all
part of the job

shit will
hit you

it'll hit you hard
and stick to
your body
for days
after your
appointment

you will want to cry
your eyes breaking
like levees in a storm

yet your body will stop you
it will be the dam
keeping everything
together

your bones a rock
there won't be
anything getting
through them

you've set your
frame up to
hold back your tears

and now you have to work
to destroy the gates

you won't have
a hammer

cement
is hard to
destroy
with your
fists

you'll have to keep
punching through
to dig up
the foundation

and most days
you'll just

want to die

as you dig
your roots up
you'll start
weaker

exhaustion will
settle inside
and you'll just
want to sleep

only

you won't
want to
wake up

your therapist
will tell you
you're not
alone

and it
will feel
like a
lifetime
before you
believe it

II

mary oliver said her lover gave her a box of darkness

said it took
years to
understand
it was a gift

when my lover
called me
a wetback

what was he
giving me

save for a
piece of
his hate

he would
hit me
with water
bottles

said i
was too
stupid
to get
smacked

he squeezed
my hands
to keep
me in
line

somedays
handholding
still
scares me

he liked to
fidget with
the bones
in my wrist

make them move
out of line

pluck my funny
bone and say
he'd paralyze
me one day

everything he
bestowed
upon me
was a gift

only i ain't
got the receipt
to return
the motherfucker

we were the calm before disaster

we stood
together
surrounded
by green
8 years ago

texas heat
washed
over us
as his head
rested on
my shoulder

statues stare
at us both
as if they know
he couldn't bear
to be held
or kissed

always a private
affair, love was
kept within
the walls
of our home

he never
smiled
but what is
there to smile
about when
happiness is an

arms reach away

the brightest moment
of our marriage
we stood together
like a calm
before turmoil
unfolded

his hail
at the gates
and my earth
waiting

as if we know
what is to come

the day i met my former father-in-law

we get to his
trailer

grass untidy

sewage line
busted

his cowboy boots
shown bright
in the alabama sun

he musta thought
i'd appreciate
them as a texan

but

i only
thought
they looked
stupid as
fuck

he lowered
his sunglasses
stared me
right in
the jaw

and said

"so you're
dating a
mexican"

my partner
at the time
grabbed
my hand
and told him

"he's one
of the
good ones"

he only snorted
and waved us
inside

my ex says some people woke up on the wrong side of the world

(shit he said when we were together)

that we all carry
pigments of flesh
and that race
never existed

when i tell him
that's about
the stupidest
shit i ever
heard

he slams his
fist into
his desk

and

tells me
to shut up

my ex tells me to be more tolerant

says i should
listen to
all sides

before judging
white people
for voting
trump

i tell him
ain't no
conservative
touchin' me
with their
dick

he says that's
the problem
"people of
color are
too closed
minded for
peace"

and i point
to our riots
i point to
all the people
killed by cops

he said this
was a matter

of class

a matter that
affected poor
white
conservatives too

and i can't help
that some people
are brainwashed
into a cult
of destruction

so i tell him
that's why
the klan
exists

right?

to help terrorize
people of color

and help
the poor
white people
who need it?

and before
he signs off
he tells me

to stop
playing

34

   identity politics

   that everyone
   is equal

   #bullshit

you texted me drunk

said you liked my pictures
that my new lover
looked perfect
at my side

asked if we planned
our photos
'cause some
of our porn pics
had to be planned

and I know you probably
felt this was all in good
innocent fun

but I wonder
what devil
rode the river
of your blood

was it my cock
you were looking at
was it jealousy
when you looked
at his eyes

what is disconnected
inside you to stay
infatuated with something
you cannot have anymore

i gave you all

the love the sky
had to offer
and you tossed
me into waiting bookshelves
and walls peeling from
your anger

you texted me
to say you still
loved me

and though you
never said it

i know how easy
words of poison
lie dormant
like a snake

waiting to
strike

when your ex says he's sorry

he says he didn't
realize how hard
it was to work

that he never understood
why i could complain
when i got home
until he actually
got a job
and worked
a full week

said the job
gave him time
to "reflect"

what the fuck
did you think
i was doing
all those hours
i was gone?

i see you
motherfucker
that you are

you are an
olympic gold
when it comes
to mental gymnastics

but i see you

as you as you are

scared boy
not yet made
it down the road
to single life

so, what do you
expect of me
great lab rat
of the past

what are you
hiding behind
your words

because you don't
say thanks unless
you want something

and i got
nothin'
more

to offer
you

i had a therapist that said he was gonna fuck me up

my husband liked
to hurt himself

when i tried
to stop him
he threw me
into a bookshelf

the bed

the wall

he's hit me
before
,
manipulated
me into
thinking
i'm the
problem in
our relationship

that we don't
fuck enough
is because
my dick don't work

my husband joked
that he'll sell
me for a peso

because that's

all i'm worth

when i told him
to seek therapy
he did

we used
the same
therapist
only

I'm lectured in
my next
session
because the
stress i put
on my husband
is affecting
his health

i'm pushed
to keep the
marriage
going because
god hates
divorce

he talks about me
in third person
says "weasel
can't man up
and talk to his
husband because
he's too tired"

says we all
tired but
we still
got a duty
to our spouse

and when i ask
how much more
can i even
give

he says
until
you have

nothing

clive barker taught me fear is everywhere

i'm lying
on the couch

snow taps the window
as i beg for sleep
to wash over me

only tonight
slumber is a beast
not ready to appear

lights out
i feel it
touching my
shoulder

but i can't see it
this invisible
grip that pushes
me between
the cracks

i can't breathe
my fingers twitch
but i can't move

i am a stone
lingering in a
pond meant
to drown me

and before i

sunk further
into the ether

it whispered to me

"i am you
i am always
there"

III

buddy wakefield taught me to look

because bodies are
as brittle as
you make
them

he says fall

fall as if you
put your
best foot
forward

knowing
mercy waits
at the bottom

yet trust is a trickster
beautiful when you
hold it, yet slippery
when your core
is off balance

when he says
"soon we will say
what we have to say
to each other's faces"

i think about you

i think about
all the things
i have yet to say

& wonder if
it's worth
the effort
to spill
those
words

the baker talks to himself while waiting

you have to mix
the eggs in
just right

'cause fuck
all if they're
at the wrong
temperature

baking is a science
dealing in precision

all details
carrying an
important limb
for the cake

take one out
and the bake
falls flat

or is denser
than your ex
gas lighting
under the moon

remember how his
words muddied
your skull?

you get frustrated
when the order

doesn't make sense

when the minuscule
become the important
your skull rattles

what cakes
do you offer
tonight?

what rage did
you pour into
the batter
to make it
as sweet?

what ingredient
did you leave
behind this time?

you were never
keen on paying
attention to
the small things

you were only
keen on making
the end stick

like sugar
to glass

orion hunts in the swamps of texas

because the stars have held him in place for
too long. cursed to fight the beast that killed him
he dips down to the earth and walks the waters
for fresh game, but what beasts can stand a man
fueled with alcohol and a bow stuck in
time? the gators are barely a match, and
the coyotes have all but run from the
immortal man. still, the beast waits above.

orion could kill the whole wetlands and
when he returned to the stars, he would find
his enemy waiting for another
round. his blade not sharp enough to pierce the
scorpion plotting his demise, he sighs,
and prays to escape the coming limbo.

sylvia plath says dying is an art

everything dies
frozen
as if covered
in snow

i want to say
winter is coming
but how can
you foresee
something
that never left

she sits by the window
sun rising over
frosted glass

says she doesn't
believe i'm real
yet she is the one
who is a ghost
in my home

sylvia tells me
everyone is a ghost

i tell her you
have to die
to become a
spirit

and she says
everything supernatural

is a result of madness

and we are all mad
waiting in boxes
to forget time
to forget peace

they like to call when the sun ain't out

from the kitchen
i see the snow
stick to the window

dawn asks for
5 more minutes
and i make coffee
while the phone
buzzes against
a pile of books

i like my
coffee acidic

it helps conjure
a spirit wicked enough
to answer vultures
on the other line

how else to handle
voices frothing
for bills unpaid

the ghost of donations long past

he ties the bracelet around our hand
says we'll become
a native by wearing it

rain overhead

we stood soaked
as a lady yells
to braid our hair

eyes watch us
from the straw market
its darkened core
towering behind
the man and his jewelry

taxi drivers behind us
pushers of blow
liquor stores
and people

surround us

we were the meat
and they were hungry

he asks for a donation
and we have nothing

no coins or bills
to give for the tired
effort of tying twine

to wrist

he curses us
under his breath
unties the bracelet

and waits for another
tourist with cash

my mother died when she wished her children normal

couldn't pull
the queer from
my spine

she spent days
tattooing
bible verses
to my skull

would turn monster
when they wouldn't
stick anymore

she had visions
for her kids

christmas movie
god lovin'
grandchildren
hetero-fantasies
were all she
ever talked about

her children were
trophies until
the gay bled out

she couldn't
pray that shit
away but goddamn

did she ever try

now she just
saves face

sits at her
kitchen table
judging from afar

my mother died
when i was a child

said her children
were too weird
to be her children

asked god
why she
couldn't have
normal ones

i never
asked her
if he answered

IV

virginia woolf steals the window in my home

she says our
worst disasters
lie within
ourselves

types at her
typewriter
as i tell her
we are all
haunted

that madness
is easy
to fall
into

woolf stares
through
the glass

trying to find
the words
to describe
winter in spring

she lets exhaustion
leave her breath
and says

madness
remakes
us

the enchantment of the ordinary

i was packing boxes
all with things
that were
easily
replaceable

kerouac in the first box
plath in the fourth
blending with
journals filled
with scraps
forgotten

but then i
found him

a fierce devil
in life
i cradled
his ashes
when i picked
him up from
the shelf

i could still hear him
yapping on cool
november mornings
waiting to be fed

i longed for him again
for the small pup
eager to bark

my ears away
because all little
cricks were a danger

what would he think
of these boxes now?
scattered like a used
bookstore, piles of
unorganized things

he wouldn't know
what psalms were
in these boxes

or that ginsberg
once had a poem
about crying

and yet i was crying
because among
all these maniacally
ordinary things

he wasn't here

i placed his ashes
on the shelf

i wasn't ready to
box him yet

i'll be damned if i didn't hit a fuckin' pole

rain in
the distance

we pull into
a gas station
inside texarkana

tank of the driver side
i turned the beast slow

like a walrus
inching its body
to go back

you had just woken up
wondering how far
'til we reach
the impossible
texas boarder

and before i could answer
our truck shook
like a tire popping

metal scratching
against the spire

i hop out the truck
curse myself as i
looked at the side
nestled firmly
against the pole

we drove through arkansas

and i remember
wondering

what the fuck
was in arkansas
aside from grass
road, and sky

two hours later
i realized

there was nothing

save for a
gas station

with a weird
bathroom

and a subway

when a texan first sees snow

i had never seen
cocaine fall
from the sky

but it was
coming down
hard

my eyes grew heavy
the further
into michigan
we drove

flakes of
snow landed
on our windshield
as the truck
slid on iced
asphalt

my things
shuffle
in the back
and i
wonder
how starless
it stays
in this state

we pull over
to a rest stop
snow sticking

to the ground

i sit back
keep the heat blasting
and watch as this
new life falls
into my lap

when poseidon drinks

i don't miss
the texas floods

but goddamn
do i miss
the rain

as if poseidon
commanded
the skies
with aggression

and pummeled
the fields
on long
summer
nights

i often dreamt
of the sea deity
tossing lightning
at god on drunk nights

as if to
drive him
out of the
megachurches

but monopolies
are hard to
destroy when
believers

fuck their
bibles into
their families

i dreamt of him
as jealous
commanding only
water while
a monster sits
on a throne
eager to erupt
in anger

but god staked
his claim on
all land

he don't share
it with nobody

not even
his son

charon likes to get out

it gets daunting
seeing the dead
flock in waives

no coins to
their ghosts

the navigator
takes his time
in texas when
the waters rise

sailing hurricanes
provides an
adventures
uncharted for
the ferryman
bound to styx

when harvey hit
i wonder what
destruction he
witnessed

did he count
the dead he
would guide

or did he
look away

as if his job

was not a
part of him

V

bukowski taught me how to fuck

admittedly not the best teacher
nor the best lover

he kept getting
lost in sadness
thinking life
is Novocain
for the leap
into death

sex as meaningful
as love

as meaningless
as beer

trapped in layers
of meaning
leading nowhere
because the cynic
can do no more
than get drunk
off what it means
to feel and be nothing

when i tied you
to the bed
he would fail
to see the heart
shape of your ass

or how your eyes

begged for me
to enter you

or how your
cock curved
back to me
as you lie
open

bukowski loves
best from
a distance

but why stay
at shore
when your waters
are so tempting

he says not
to undress
love

that the words
that form it
are a cavern
unfulfilled

but I'll strip
it apart

take every letter
of your body
til i reach the core

bukowski taught me
how to fuck

stripped meaning away
and left hell
intact

what he failed
to see was
we're all full
moons

all voids
waiting

to be
devoured

i read a poem about eating your ass to my friends

the drum circle was tacky
and unbalanced

like raindrops
slowing
from a
dying storm

first to read
these straights
ain't never been
hit with so much
tongue fucking
and dicks

and

acrobatics or restraints

but they asked for it

said all sex is beautiful
when what they meant
to say was keep that
shit locked up

don't nobody want
to know what happens
in bedrooms unexplored

mouths and assholes
should never join hands

yet when my tongue
set foot on your earth

weary traveler that it was

i only felt eager
to navigate the rivers
of your curves

they said they
wanted intimacy

what's more fucking
intimate than learning
the trails of your legs
or the softness
of your belly

or the whines
raining from your lips
as my tongue splits you open

how boring is their sex life
that they're so embarrassed by ours

first to read
first to leave

an exit fitting
of a fag
among people
un-queer

the sun was setting as we left port

warm for winter
a breeze smoothed
against us as
we sat on the balcony

the ship played
a song as we departed

but i'll be damned
if i knew what it was

ocean air covered
the noise as we
moved further
away from miami

and when the first
stars arrived
i kissed you

the sea at our backs
i pulled you close
as buildings
faded

to twilight

what if i never get rid of you

they ask

as if it were
the worst thing
that could happen
in my life

and i want
to tell them
that death
could climb
into my bed

possess my body
wreck my bones

leave me
 a disaster
fitting for
texas

and

i'd still crawl
through hades
to be with Eros
for eternity

arthur c. clarke taught me how to wonder

that dreaming honest
is less hobby
than planning

pushing the waters
to find boundaries
unknown while
putting light years
to words

what friend is comfort
when distant earths
lie restless & waiting

each decade is a childhood
they all end abruptly
as the new is ushered in

when you tapped into my timeline
what new earth did you plan
on shaping at the core
of the dilapidated

lover

we hopped in a car
drove 40+ hours
to a new life

yet I still wonder what
the next 7 months
will look like

the next 7 years

what stars lie beyond
the boundary of time

you put the brightest star on top

tangled tinsel
and lights
like a snake
wrapped in
branches

eros
the giver

presents sit underneath
all land mines
waiting to be
discovered

waiting to burst
in front of their
new owner

i'd say my Christmas
trees are long past

and you'd only say
fuck that
and fuck the "sorry"
that would spill from
my lips shortly after

all while dancing
to Mariah Carrie
in our living room

you know me too well

lover

but i guess that's how
rejuvenation works

by throwing yourself
to the top
where all the light
dances to clear
the debris
of past lives

long
dead

we kissed beneath a streetlight

on the first
night back

after hours
of driving
from the
warm depths
of the south

to the cold
grasp of
northern snow

the air grazed
our cheeks

we were home

outro

healing is a slit throat waiting to sing

i keep wanting
to dig my
coffin early

as if being
late to my
funeral
is a tragedy
my ghost can't
handle

death is magnetic
pulling on your
wounds
to return
you to
soil

some nights
i see the
grave i
dug
and
howl under
full moons
because i'm
not ready
to own
my traumas

and i ask myself
when will i be

but my skull
is a collection
of noise

pulling an
answer is
like grabbing
fistfuls of
mismatched
screws in
search of the
right one

only

they're all stripped
and bent sideways

i get lost

a lot

navigating the
forest of my
past is a hike
all too new

i've been
stuck there
trying to
get gone

yet all i find

is a coffin
at the edge

one I'm teetering
the edge of
lying inside

Other Titles by Weasel

Poetry
Born Into This
a warm place to self-destruct
We Don't Make It Out Alive
Cut the Loss
Time Passes Like Flames in the Distance
We Balanced Gravity As I Ate You Out

Fiction
Cigarette Burns
We Live for Half-Moons
Jazz at the End of the Night
Carnage

Film
Poetry is Dead

Editor of
#ohmurr!
Body & Blood
Blood, Sweat and Fists
Degenerates: Voices for Peace
Difursity
Dread
Furnicate
The Haunted Traveler
How Well You Walk Through Madness
Incendiary
Knotted
Ordinary Madness
Passing Through
Purrgatorio
Typewriter Emergencies
Vagabonds: Anthology of the Mad Ones

Weasel is a queer, biracial author and The Dude of Weasel Press. He is the editor of Vagabonds: Anthology of the Mad Ones, Body & Blood, #ohmurr, and several other anthologies. As an editor and as a writer, Weasel likes to focus on pushing the boundaries of queer and sex positive subjects. He maintains a blog of his personal and sexual experiences, as well as his experiences with domestic abuse. Weasel's work has been featured in a few anthologies, some of which include: SickLit magazine, 13 Poets, Harbinger Asylum, Di-Verse-City, Sensory Details, Sinister Sheets, and several others. In 2016 and 2019, he was selected to be a Juried Poet for the Houston Poetry Festival. He is also a book blogger who reviews horror, erotica, and poetry. You can follow Weasel at the information below:

Twitter: @systmaticweasel
Adult (NSFW) Twitter: @systmaticwzl
Instagram: @systmaticwzl

https://www.facebook.com/poetweasel
https://degenerateweasel.weebly.com
https://queerweasel.blogspot.com
https://hellstoatreviews.weebly.com

OTHER TITLES FROM WEASEL PRESS

Pan's Saxophone by Jonel Abellanosa
Hyper-Real Reboots by Sudeep Adhikari
despair is a mandelbrot set by Sudeep Adhikari
Wayward Realm by Sendokidu Adomi
Ghost Train by Matt Borczon
To Burn in Torturous Algorithms by Heath Brougher
Klonopin Meets Sisyphus by Adam Levon Brown
Harmonious Anarchy by Matthew David Campbell
H A I L by Stanford Cheung
Young Thieves in a Growing Orchard by Samuel E. Cole
Talk Like Jazz by Joseph Cooper
The Madness of Empty Spaces by David E. Cowen
The Seven Yards of Sorrow by David E. Cowen
Bleeding Saffron by David E. Cowen
Face Down in the Leaves by Dwale
Wine Country by Robin Wyatt Dunn
City, Psychonaut by Robin Wyatt Dunn
Dark is a Color of the Day by Robin Wyatt Dunn
Smash & Grab Poems by Ryan Quinn Flanagan
In Winter's Dreams We Wake by Ryan Quinn Flanagan
Improbable...Never Impossible by Vixyy Fox
Reach for the Sky by Vixyy Fox
The Night at the End of the Tunnel or Isaiah Can You See? by Mark Greenside
Brinwood by RK Gold
Just Under the Sky by RK Gold
Civilized Beasts Vol I-III edited by Laura Govednik
If the Hero of Time was Black by Ashley Harris
Furry Haiku edited by Thurston Howl
Dormant Volcano by Ken Jones
Email Epistles by Ken Jones
In and of Blood by Kat Lewis
Purple Fantasies by Gary Mielo
Evergreen by Sarah Frances Moran
I Am A Terrorist by Sarah Frances Moran
Death & Heartbreak by Leah Mueller
Blame it On the Texas Sky by Max Mundan
I'll Only Write Poems for You by Max Mundan
Rising from the Ashes by Meghan O'Hern
Lipstick Stained Masculinity by Mason O'Hern

Chaos Songs by Scott Thomas Outlar
Viscera by Manna Plourde
Ribbon and Leviathan by Manna Plourde
In Another Life, Maybe by Michael Prihoda
the first breath you take after giving up by Michael Prihoda
the same that happened yesterday by Michael Prihoda
Beneath this Planetarium by Michael Prihoda
Years without Room by Michael Prihoda
Toast is Just Bread that Put Up A Fight by Emily Ramser
I forgot How To Write When They Diagnosed Me by Emily Ramser
Conjuring Her by Emily Ramser
UHAUL: A Collection of Lesbian Love Poems by Emily Ramser
The Escape by Rayah
Miffed and Peeved in the UK by Neil S. Reddy
Taxi Sam in PINK NOIR by Neil S. Reddy
Not Kafka: A Collection of Ugly Shorts by Neil S. Reddy
Tales in Liquid Time by Neil S. Reddy
Inevitable by Amy L. Sasser
Taste I Say, You're Timeless by Chuck Taylor
Blood Criminals: Living with HIV in 21st Century America by Jonathan W. Thurston
Satan's Sweethearts by Marge Simon and Mary Turzillo
We Don't Make It Out Alive by Weasel
Cut the Loss by Weasel
Jazz at the End of the Night by Weasel
Time Passes Like Flames in the Distance by Weasel
Vagabonds: Anthology of the Mad Ones edited by Weasel
Passing Through edited by Weasel
How Well You Walk Through Madness edited by Weasel
Colliding with Orion by Chris Wise
Wolf: An Epic and Other Poems by Z.M. Wise
Kosmish and the Horned Ones by Z.M. Wise

www.ingramcontent.com/pod-product-compliance
Lightning Source LLC
Chambersburg PA
CBHW051658040426
42446CB00009B/1191